The Future of AI

of AI

Neil King

How Machine Learning Will Change Business Forever

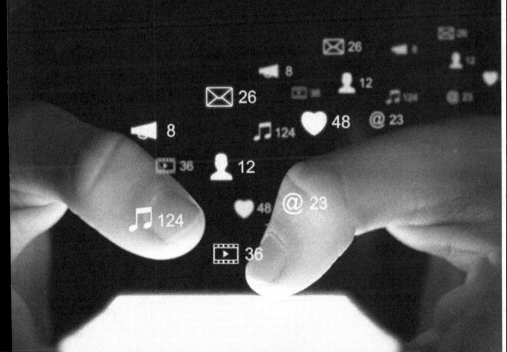

Introduction

Definition of AI and Machine Learning

Artificial Intelligence (AI) and Machine Learning (ML) are two of the most talked-about technologies in the world today. They are rapidly transforming the way we live, work, and interact with technology. Although the terms are often used interchangeably, they are not the same thing. In this subchapter, we will define AI and Machine Learning and explore how they are changing the world of business.

AI is the simulation of human intelligence processes by machines, especially computer systems. It involves the creation of intelligent machines that can work and think like humans. These machines can learn, reason, plan, and perceive. AI is concerned with building systems that can perform tasks that would usually require human intelligence, such as speech recognition, decision making, and natural language processing.

Machine Learning, on the other hand, is a subset of AI. It is the process of teaching machines to learn from data, without being explicitly programmed. Machine Learning algorithms enable machines to learn from experience, just like humans do. They can identify patterns and relationships in data, and use this knowledge to make predictions or decisions.

AI and Machine Learning are transforming the world of business in several ways. They are enabling companies to automate repetitive tasks, improve customer experiences, and make better decisions. For example, businesses can use Machine Learning algorithms to analyze customer data and gain insights into their behaviors and preferences. This information can then be used to create personalized marketing campaigns and improve customer retention.

However, AI and Machine Learning also pose significant cybersecurity risks. As these technologies become more sophisticated, they can be used for malicious purposes, such as hacking, fraud, and cyber attacks. Therefore, businesses must implement robust cybersecurity measures to protect their data and systems from these threats.

In conclusion, AI and Machine Learning are transforming the world of business and technology. They are creating new opportunities for innovation and growth, but also pose significant cybersecurity risks. As these technologies continue to evolve, it is essential for businesses to stay informed and adapt to the changing landscape.

Importance of AI and Machine Learning in Business

In today's digital age, businesses are constantly looking for ways to stay ahead of the competition. And, with the advent of Artificial Intelligence (AI) and Machine Learning (ML), companies have found a new weapon to help them do just that. AI and ML are revolutionizing the way businesses operate, and their importance cannot be overstated.

One of the key advantages of AI and ML is their ability to analyze large amounts of data quickly and accurately. This can help businesses make better decisions, improve customer service, and increase productivity. For example, AI can analyze customer data to identify patterns and preferences, which can be used to personalize marketing efforts and improve customer experience. Similarly, ML can analyze manufacturing data to optimize production processes, reduce waste, and increase efficiency.

Another important benefit of AI and ML is their ability to automate repetitive tasks. This can free up employees to focus on more strategic tasks, such as innovation, creativity, and problem-solving. For example, AI can automate data entry, scheduling, and report generation, while ML can automate fraud detection, cybersecurity, and predictive maintenance.

AI and ML can also help businesses stay ahead of the curve by identifying emerging trends and predicting future events. This can be invaluable in industries such as finance, where predicting market trends and making accurate investment decisions is critical. Similarly, in healthcare, AI and ML can help identify disease outbreaks and predict patient outcomes, which can help healthcare providers make better decisions.

Of course, with all the benefits that AI and ML offer, there are also risks. Cybersecurity is one of the biggest concerns, as AI and ML systems can be vulnerable to hacking and other cyber threats. However, with proper security measures in place, the benefits of AI and ML far outweigh the risks.

In conclusion, AI and ML are transforming the way businesses operate, and their importance cannot be overstated. By analyzing data, automating tasks, and predicting future events, AI and ML can help businesses make better decisions, improve customer service, and increase productivity. However, it is important to be aware of the risks and take steps to ensure that AI and ML systems are secure. The future of business is here, and it is powered by AI and ML.

Purpose of the Book

The purpose of this book is to provide a comprehensive overview of the future of AI and how machine learning will change business forever. The world is rapidly evolving, and technology is playing a significant role in shaping our future. Artificial intelligence technology is poised to play a vital role in the future of business, and cybersecurity technology is becoming more critical than ever.

The book is aimed at a trade audience interested in technology and business and the future of the world. The niche audience of technology, Artificial intelligence technology, and Cybersecurity technology will find this book highly informative and valuable. The book aims to provide a clear understanding of the current state of AI technology and its future potential. It will explore how machine learning is transforming various industries and how businesses can harness the power of AI to drive growth, innovation, and competitive advantage.

The book will also delve into the ethical and social implications of AI and how businesses can address these challenges. It will examine how AI can be used to improve cybersecurity and protect against cyber threats. The book will provide real-world examples of how AI is already being used in business and industry, as well as predictions for the future.

The book is written by experts in the field of AI, technology, and business, providing readers with a deep understanding of the subject matter. The authors have extensive experience in the industry and have worked with some of the most innovative companies in the world. Their insights and analysis will provide readers with a unique perspective on the future of AI and its impact on business and society.

In conclusion, the purpose of this book is to provide a comprehensive overview of the future of AI and how machine learning will change business forever. It is aimed at a trade audience interested in technology and business and the future of the world, and the niches of technology, Artificial intelligence technology, and Cybersecurity technology. The book aims to provide readers with a clear understanding of the current state of AI technology and its future potential, as well as exploring the ethical and social implications of AI, and how businesses can harness the power of AI to drive growth and innovation.

The Current State of AI

Overview of AI and Machine Learning in Business

Artificial intelligence (AI) and machine learning (ML) are rapidly transforming the way businesses operate. From automating mundane tasks to making complex decisions, businesses of all sizes are leveraging AI and ML to gain a competitive edge in their respective industries.

The use of AI and ML in business is not a new concept. However, recent advancements in the technology have made it more accessible and affordable than ever before. From chatbots and virtual assistants to predictive analytics and fraud detection, AI and ML are being applied to a wide range of business functions.

One of the key benefits of using AI and ML in business is the ability to automate repetitive tasks. This not only saves time but also reduces the risk of human error. For example, chatbots can handle customer queries and complaints, freeing up customer support staff to focus on more complex issues.

Another important application of AI and ML in business is predictive analytics. By analyzing large volumes of data, businesses can gain insights into customer behavior, market trends, and other key factors that impact their bottom line. This can help businesses make informed decisions about product development, marketing strategies, and more.

AI and ML are also playing a significant role in cybersecurity. With cyber threats becoming more sophisticated and frequent, businesses are turning to AI and ML to proactively identify and mitigate potential breaches. This includes using machine learning algorithms to analyze network traffic and identify anomalies that could indicate a cyber attack.

Overall, the use of AI and ML in business is rapidly changing the way organizations operate. From improving efficiency and reducing costs to enhancing decision-making capabilities and bolstering cybersecurity, the potential benefits are vast. As the technology continues to evolve, businesses that embrace AI and ML will be better positioned to thrive in an increasingly competitive and fast-paced marketplace.

Advancements in AI technology

Advancements in AI Technology

As machine learning continues to evolve, we are witnessing incredible advancements in AI technology that are changing the way we live, work, and interact with the world around us. From self-driving cars to virtual assistants, AI technology is transforming the business landscape and revolutionizing the way we approach cybersecurity.

One of the most exciting advancements in AI technology is the development of natural language processing (NLP), which enables machines to understand and interpret human language. This breakthrough has led to the creation of virtual assistants like Siri, Alexa, and Google Assistant, which can understand complex commands and respond in real-time. NLP technology is also being used to improve customer service and support, allowing businesses to provide more personalized and efficient service to their customers.

Another area of AI technology that is rapidly advancing is computer vision, which enables machines to interpret and analyze visual information. This technology is being used in a range of applications, from facial recognition to self-driving cars. With computer vision, machines can identify objects, analyze patterns, and make decisions in real-time based on visual data.

Advancements in AI technology are also having a significant impact on cybersecurity. As cyber threats continue to evolve, AI technology is being used to detect and respond to threats in real-time. Machine learning algorithms can analyze vast amounts of data to identify patterns and anomalies that may indicate a security breach. This technology is also being used to develop predictive analytics, which can help businesses anticipate and prevent cyber attacks before they occur.

In conclusion, the advancements in AI technology are set to transform the business landscape and the way we approach cybersecurity. From virtual assistants to self-driving cars, AI technology is changing the way we live and work. As we continue to explore the possibilities of machine learning, we can expect even more exciting developments in the future.

Current Applications of AI in Business

AI has already started making its presence felt in the world of business, and the trend is only going to continue. From automating mundane tasks to decision-making and customer engagement, AI has the potential to transform the way businesses operate. Here are some of the current applications of AI in business:

1. Chatbots - Chatbots are AI-powered conversational agents that can be used to provide customer support and assistance. They can handle simple queries, resolve customer issues, and even take orders. Chatbots are available 24/7 and can handle multiple customer interactions simultaneously, making them a valuable asset for businesses.

2. Personalization - AI can help businesses personalize their marketing and sales efforts. By analyzing customer data, AI algorithms can identify patterns and preferences and provide personalized recommendations. This can improve customer engagement and increase sales.

3. Fraud detection - AI can be used to detect fraudulent activities in real-time. By analyzing transaction data, AI algorithms can identify suspicious behavior and flag it for further investigation. This can help businesses prevent financial losses due to fraudulent activities.

4. Cybersecurity - AI can help businesses protect their networks and systems from cyber attacks. By analyzing network traffic, AI algorithms can identify potential threats and take preventive measures. AI can also be used to detect and respond to attacks in real-time, minimizing the damage caused.

5. Predictive analytics - AI can be used to predict future trends and outcomes based on historical data. By analyzing customer data, sales data, and market trends, AI algorithms can identify patterns and make predictions about future events. This can help businesses make informed decisions and stay ahead of the competition.

These are just some of the current applications of AI in business. As AI technology continues to advance, we can expect to see more innovative use cases and new business models emerge. Businesses that embrace AI and incorporate it into their operations will be better positioned to succeed in the future.

The Benefits and Challenges of AI

The Benefits and Challenges of AI

Artificial Intelligence (AI) is transforming the world around us and disrupting almost every industry. It is fundamentally changing the way businesses operate and the way we live our lives. AI offers numerous benefits that can improve efficiency, productivity, and profitability. However, it also presents several challenges that need to be addressed.

Benefits of AI

1. Increased Efficiency: AI-based systems can perform repetitive tasks quickly and accurately, freeing up human resources for more critical and creative tasks.

2. Improved Decision Making: AI systems can analyze vast amounts of data to make informed decisions and predictions. This can help businesses make better decisions and stay ahead of the competition.

3. Customized User Experience: AI-based systems can personalize user experiences by analyzing user data and preferences. This can lead to more satisfied customers and increased loyalty.

4. Enhanced Cybersecurity: AI-based cybersecurity systems can detect and prevent cyber threats faster and more effectively than traditional methods.

5. Cost Reduction: AI can automate many tasks, leading to reduced labor costs and increased profitability.

Challenges of AI

1. Job Displacement: AI-based automation may lead to job losses in certain industries, which can have a significant impact on the workforce.

2. Bias and Discrimination: AI systems can be biased based on the data they are trained on, leading to discrimination against certain groups.

3. Privacy Concerns: AI systems can collect vast amounts of user data, potentially compromising privacy.

4. Lack of Accountability: AI systems are not infallible and can make mistakes. It is essential to have accountability measures in place to address any errors or malfunctions.

5. Ethical Concerns: AI systems can be used for unethical purposes, such as creating deepfakes or manipulating public opinion.

Conclusion

AI has the potential to transform the way we live and work. It can bring numerous benefits that can improve efficiency, productivity, and profitability. However, it also presents several challenges that need to be addressed. It is essential to develop ethical and responsible AI systems that can positively impact society while avoiding negative consequences. The future of AI is bright, but it requires a thoughtful and deliberate approach to ensure its benefits are maximized while minimizing its challenges.

The Future of AI

The Potential of AI in Business

The Potential of AI in Business

Artificial intelligence (AI) is revolutionizing the way businesses operate. From enhancing customer experiences to streamlining business processes, AI is transforming the business landscape. The potential of AI in business is limitless, and its impact on the future of the world is significant. In this subchapter, we will explore the potential of AI in business and its implications for the future.

One of the most significant benefits of AI in business is its ability to improve the customer experience. AI-powered chatbots and virtual assistants are increasingly being used by businesses to provide 24/7 customer support. These AI-powered chatbots can handle a wide range of customer inquiries, from answering simple questions to resolving complex issues. This not only improves customer satisfaction but also reduces the workload on customer support teams.

AI is also transforming the way businesses make decisions. AI algorithms can analyze vast amounts of data and provide insights that would be impossible for humans to uncover. This enables businesses to make data-driven decisions quickly, improving operational efficiency and profitability.

Another area where AI is making a significant impact is in cybersecurity. AI-powered cybersecurity solutions can detect and respond to threats in real-time, reducing the risk of data breaches. This is particularly important for businesses that handle sensitive customer data, such as financial institutions and healthcare providers.

AI is also transforming the way businesses operate. For example, AI-powered automation can streamline business processes, reducing the need for manual labor. This not only improves efficiency but also reduces errors and improves quality.

In conclusion, the potential of AI in business is vast. From enhancing customer experiences to improving operational efficiency and profitability, AI is transforming the business landscape. However, as with any new technology, there are also risks and challenges associated with AI. Businesses must be aware of these risks and take steps to mitigate them. Overall, the future of AI in business looks bright, and its impact on the future of the world is significant.

Predictions for the Future of AI

The future of AI is an exciting and rapidly evolving field that has the potential to revolutionize the world as we know it. From self-driving cars to intelligent robots, AI has the power to transform industries and change the way we live and work.

One prediction for the future of AI is that it will continue to advance at an exponential rate. As more data becomes available and algorithms become more sophisticated, AI systems will become more powerful and capable of handling increasingly complex tasks.

Another prediction is that AI will become more integrated into our daily lives. From virtual assistants like Siri and Alexa to smart homes and self-driving cars, AI will become a ubiquitous part of our daily routines.

However, with great power comes great responsibility, and one of the biggest challenges facing the future of AI is cybersecurity. As AI systems become more sophisticated and ubiquitous, they will also become more vulnerable to cyber attacks. It is essential that we develop robust cybersecurity measures to protect these systems and prevent them from being used for malicious purposes.

Finally, the future of AI will also be shaped by ethical and moral considerations. As AI systems become more intelligent and autonomous, they will also become more capable of making decisions on their own. It is essential that we establish clear ethical guidelines for the development and use of AI to ensure that it is used for the benefit of society as a whole.

In conclusion, the future of AI is an exciting and rapidly evolving field with enormous potential to transform the world. However, it is essential that we approach this technology with caution, and carefully consider the ethical, moral, and cybersecurity implications of its development and use. With the right approach, AI has the power to revolutionize the world and change the way we live and work for the better.

The Impact of AI on Employment

The Impact of AI on Employment

Artificial Intelligence (AI) has been a buzzword in the tech industry for some time now, and it's not difficult to see why. The potential of AI to transform business processes and create new products and services is enormous. However, one area that often gets overlooked in discussions about AI is its impact on employment. In this section, we'll explore the ways in which AI is changing the world of work and what that means for businesses and employees.

The rise of AI has led to fears that it could replace human workers, leading to mass unemployment and economic upheaval. While it's true that AI is capable of automating many tasks that were previously performed by humans, it's important to note that it's not a one-size-fits-all solution. AI is best suited to tasks that are repetitive and require a high degree of precision, such as data entry or quality control. However, there are many tasks that are best performed by humans, such as creative problem-solving or tasks that require empathy and emotional intelligence.

One of the key benefits of AI is that it can free up human workers to focus on tasks that require their unique skills and expertise. For example, a customer service chatbot may be able to handle basic queries, freeing up human representatives to handle more complex issues. This can lead to a more efficient and effective workforce, as well as an improved customer experience.

However, there are also challenges associated with the rise of AI. One of the biggest is the potential for job displacement. As AI becomes more sophisticated, it's likely that it will be able to perform tasks that were previously thought to be the exclusive domain of humans. This could lead to job losses in certain industries, particularly those that rely heavily on manual labor or routine tasks.

Another challenge is the need for retraining. As AI becomes more prevalent in the workplace, it's likely that many workers will need to learn new skills in order to remain relevant. This could be a particular challenge for older workers, who may find it more difficult to adapt to new technologies.

Finally, there are concerns about the impact of AI on cybersecurity. As AI becomes more sophisticated, it's likely that cybercriminals will also use it to develop more sophisticated attacks. This could lead to a greater need for cybersecurity professionals, as well as increased investment in cybersecurity technology.

In conclusion, the impact of AI on employment is complex and multifaceted. While there are certainly challenges associated with the rise of AI, there are also many opportunities. Businesses that are able to harness the power of AI while also investing in their human workforce are likely to be the most successful in the long run.

Ethical Concerns of AI in Business

The rise of artificial intelligence (AI) has brought about many changes in the business world. While AI has the potential to revolutionize various industries, it also raises ethical concerns that need to be addressed. In this subchapter, we will explore the ethical concerns of AI in business and how they can be mitigated.

One of the primary ethical concerns of AI in business is the potential for bias. AI systems are only as unbiased as the data they are trained on. If the data used to train the AI system is biased, the system will also be biased. This could lead to discriminatory practices in hiring, lending, and other areas where AI is used. To mitigate this concern, businesses need to ensure that their data is diverse and representative of the population they serve.

Another ethical concern of AI in business is the potential for job displacement. As AI becomes more prevalent, it has the potential to replace human workers in various industries. While this could lead to increased efficiency and productivity, it could also lead to job losses and economic hardship. To address this concern, businesses need to invest in reskilling and upskilling their employees to prepare them for the jobs of the future.

Cybersecurity is also a major concern when it comes to AI in business. AI systems are vulnerable to cyber attacks, which could lead to data breaches and other security issues. To mitigate this concern, businesses need to ensure that their AI systems are secure and that they have robust cybersecurity measures in place.

Finally, there is the concern of accountability and transparency. AI systems are often opaque, and it can be challenging to understand how they make decisions. This could lead to issues of accountability and transparency, especially in high-stakes situations such as healthcare and criminal justice. To address this concern, businesses need to ensure that their AI systems are transparent and that they can be audited and explained.

In conclusion, the ethical concerns of AI in business need to be addressed to ensure that AI is used responsibly and ethically. By investing in diverse data, reskilling employees, ensuring cybersecurity, and promoting accountability and transparency, businesses can mitigate these concerns and use AI to drive innovation and growth.

Machine Learning in Business

Overview of Machine Learning in Business

Machine learning has become an integral part of the business landscape, and it has the potential to revolutionize the way companies operate. Machine learning is a subset of artificial intelligence that enables systems to learn and improve from experience without being explicitly programmed. With the vast amount of data available, machine learning algorithms can identify patterns, predict outcomes, and make informed decisions.

The use of machine learning in business has led to increased efficiency, improved decision-making, and reduced costs. Companies can use machine learning to analyze large datasets and identify trends that would be difficult or impossible for humans to identify. Machine learning algorithms can also identify anomalies and outliers that may indicate fraudulent activity or cybersecurity threats.

One of the most significant impacts of machine learning on business is the ability to personalize customer experiences. Machine learning algorithms can analyze customer data to provide personalized recommendations, targeted marketing campaigns, and customized product offerings. This level of personalization can increase customer loyalty and satisfaction, leading to increased revenue.

Another area where machine learning has significant potential is in cybersecurity. Machine learning algorithms can analyze network traffic and identify patterns that may indicate a cyber attack. This proactive approach to cybersecurity can help companies identify threats before they become a problem, reducing the risk of data breaches and other cybersecurity incidents.

While machine learning has many benefits for business, there are also challenges to consider. One of the biggest challenges is the need for high-quality data. Machine learning algorithms require accurate and relevant data to make informed decisions. If companies do not have access to high-quality data, the algorithms may provide inaccurate or misleading results.

Another challenge is the potential for bias in machine learning algorithms. If the data used to train the algorithms is biased, the results may be biased as well. This can lead to discriminatory practices and negative impacts on certain groups of people.

In conclusion, machine learning is transforming the business landscape, with the potential to revolutionize the way companies operate. While there are challenges to consider, the benefits of machine learning are significant, including increased efficiency, improved decision-making, and reduced costs. As companies continue to adopt machine learning, it is important to consider the ethical implications and ensure that the algorithms are designed to be fair and unbiased.

Applications of Machine Learning in Business

The applications of machine learning in business have been growing rapidly in recent years. Machine learning is a subset of artificial intelligence (AI) that involves using algorithms to learn from data and make predictions or decisions.

One major application of machine learning in business is in customer service. Companies can use machine learning algorithms to analyze customer data such as purchase history, browsing behavior, and demographic information to create personalized recommendations and offers. Machine learning can also be used to automate customer service tasks such as chatbots and virtual assistants that can quickly answer customer inquiries and resolve issues.

Another application of machine learning in business is in fraud detection and cybersecurity. Machine learning algorithms can be trained on large datasets of historical fraud cases to identify patterns and anomalies that signal potential fraud. This can help financial institutions and other companies prevent fraud before it occurs, saving millions of dollars.

Machine learning is also being applied to supply chain management, where it can help optimize inventory levels, reduce waste, and improve delivery times. By analyzing data on customer demand, production capacity, and supplier performance, machine learning algorithms can help companies make better decisions about when and where to source materials and how much to order.

In the healthcare industry, machine learning is being used to improve patient outcomes and reduce costs. Machine learning algorithms can analyze patient data such as medical records, lab results, and genomics to identify patterns and predict disease risk. This can help doctors make more accurate diagnoses and develop more effective treatment plans.

Overall, the applications of machine learning in business are numerous and varied. As companies continue to collect more data and invest in AI technology, we can expect to see even more innovative uses of machine learning in the future. However, it is important to also consider the ethical implications of using machine learning in business, such as potential biases and privacy concerns, and to develop responsible AI practices to ensure that these technologies are used in a way that benefits society as a whole.

The Benefits and Challenges of Machine Learning

The Benefits and Challenges of Machine Learning

Machine learning has come to the forefront of the technology industry in recent years, and for good reason. It has the potential to revolutionize the way businesses operate, from improving customer experiences to streamlining internal processes. However, this technology is not without its challenges, and understanding both the benefits and challenges of machine learning is crucial for businesses to make informed decisions about its implementation.

Benefits of Machine Learning

Improved Efficiency: Machine learning algorithms can analyze large amounts of data and identify patterns that humans may miss, leading to more efficient processes and decision-making.

Personalization: By analyzing customer data, machine learning can create personalized experiences for customers, improving satisfaction and loyalty.

Cost Savings: By automating certain tasks, businesses can save on labor costs and improve overall efficiency.

Cybersecurity: Machine learning can be used to detect and prevent cyber attacks, as well as analyze data to identify potential vulnerabilities.

Challenges of Machine Learning

Data Bias: Machine learning algorithms are only as good as the data they are trained on. If the data used to train the algorithm is biased, the algorithm will be biased as well.

Data Privacy: The use of machine learning requires large amounts of data, which can raise concerns about data privacy and security.

Human Oversight: While machine learning can automate certain tasks, it still requires human oversight to ensure accuracy and prevent errors.

Lack of Understanding: Machine learning is a complex technology, and many businesses may not fully understand how to implement it effectively.

Conclusion

Machine learning has the potential to revolutionize the way businesses operate, but it is important to understand both the benefits and challenges of this technology. By leveraging the benefits and addressing the challenges, businesses can use machine learning to improve efficiency, personalize experiences, save costs, and enhance cybersecurity. However, businesses must also be aware of potential biases, data privacy concerns, and the need for human oversight and understanding. As machine learning continues to evolve, it will be crucial for businesses to stay informed and adapt to this rapidly changing technology.

The Future of Machine Learning in Business

The Future of Machine Learning in Business

Machine learning has already brought significant changes in the world of business and technology. With the increasing demand for data-driven decisions, machine learning is becoming an essential tool for businesses of all sizes. The future of machine learning in business is set to revolutionize how companies operate, and this technology is expected to become even more prevalent in the next few years.

One of the most significant benefits of machine learning in business is its ability to improve efficiency. With machine learning algorithms, businesses can automate mundane tasks and optimize processes, reducing the time and resources required to complete them. This, in turn, allows businesses to focus on more critical tasks and make better-informed decisions.

Another area where machine learning is expected to have a significant impact is customer service. With the increasing use of chatbots powered by machine learning algorithms, businesses can provide 24/7 customer service to their clients, reducing the need for human intervention. These chatbots can handle simple customer queries, freeing up customer service representatives to deal with more complex issues.

Machine learning is also expected to revolutionize the field of cybersecurity. With the increasing number of cyber attacks, businesses need to be proactive in protecting their data. Machine learning algorithms can help detect and analyze potential threats, allowing businesses to take preventive action and minimize the risk of data breaches.

In the coming years, machine learning is expected to become even more prevalent in the field of business. With advancements in technology, machine learning algorithms will become even more powerful, allowing businesses to make more accurate predictions and decisions.

However, there are also concerns about the impact of machine learning on the job market. As more tasks become automated, some jobs may become redundant, leading to job losses. This is a concern that needs to be addressed by businesses and policymakers alike.

In conclusion, the future of machine learning in business is promising. This technology is set to revolutionize how businesses operate, making them more efficient, customer-focused, and secure. However, it is essential to address the potential impact on the job market and ensure that the benefits of machine learning are shared equitably.

Cybersecurity and AI

Overview of Cybersecurity and AI

Overview of Cybersecurity and AI

As artificial intelligence (AI) proliferates in our lives, cybersecurity becomes a more pressing concern. The integration of AI technology in our daily lives creates new vulnerabilities that can be exploited by cybercriminals. Hence, it is crucial that we understand the relationship between AI and cybersecurity to ensure that our technological advancements are secure and reliable.

AI is a powerful tool that can help us solve complex problems, make informed decisions, and automate tasks that were once thought impossible. However, AI systems are only as good as the data they are trained on. This means that if the data is corrupted or manipulated, the AI system's output will be flawed. Cybercriminals can exploit this vulnerability to gain access to sensitive data, steal intellectual property, and cause operational disruptions.

Furthermore, AI systems can also be manipulated to generate fake news, misinformation, and deepfakes. These AI-generated content can spread like wildfire through social media, causing public panic and unrest. AI can also be used to launch sophisticated phishing attacks, where cybercriminals use AI to generate personalized messages that are indistinguishable from genuine emails.

To counter these threats, cybersecurity experts are turning to AI itself. AI can be used to detect and respond to cyber threats in real-time, identify anomalies in network traffic, and detect fraudulent activities. AI can also be used to automate cybersecurity tasks, such as vulnerability assessments, patch management, and incident response.

However, AI is not a magic bullet. AI systems are susceptible to the same vulnerabilities as traditional software, such as buffer overflow, SQL injection, and cross-site scripting. Moreover, AI systems can be biased, and the data they are trained on can reflect the biases of their creators. Therefore, it is essential to develop AI systems that are transparent, explainable, and free from bias.

In conclusion, AI and cybersecurity are two sides of the same coin. As AI becomes more prevalent in our lives, we must ensure that we have robust cybersecurity measures in place to protect our technological advancements. AI can be used to enhance cybersecurity, but we must also be aware of the vulnerabilities that AI can create. By understanding the relationship between AI and cybersecurity, we can build a safer and more secure future for all.

The Importance of Cybersecurity in AI

The Importance of Cybersecurity in AI

Artificial intelligence (AI) has already changed the way businesses operate, and its impact on the global economy is only expected to grow. AI technology is now being used to automate repetitive tasks, reduce errors and improve efficiency in various business processes. However, as the use of AI continues to expand, so do the risks associated with it. Cybersecurity is a crucial aspect of AI that businesses must pay close attention to.

One of the biggest risks associated with AI is the potential for cyber attacks. Cybercriminals can use various techniques to hack into AI systems and steal sensitive data or disrupt business operations. These attacks can be devastating to the affected organizations, resulting in significant financial losses, reputational damage, and legal liabilities.

Furthermore, AI systems are only as good as the data they are trained on. If the data is compromised, the AI system's output may be inaccurate or biased, leading to incorrect decisions. Therefore, it is essential to implement robust cybersecurity measures to ensure the integrity and confidentiality of the data used to train the AI system.

Another important aspect of cybersecurity in AI is the need to ensure that the AI system's algorithms are transparent and understandable. AI systems are often seen as black boxes, meaning that it is challenging to understand how the system arrived at a particular decision. This lack of transparency can be problematic, especially in critical decision-making scenarios. Therefore, it is crucial to ensure that AI algorithms are explainable and can be audited to ensure that they are operating as intended.

In conclusion, the importance of cybersecurity in AI cannot be overstated. As AI technology continues to evolve and become more prevalent, it is essential that businesses prioritize cybersecurity to mitigate the risks associated with it. By implementing robust cybersecurity measures, organizations can ensure the integrity and confidentiality of their data, protect themselves from cyber attacks, and ensure that AI systems operate transparently and accurately.

The Potential of AI in Cybersecurity

The Potential of AI in Cybersecurity

As technology continues to advance, the threat of cyber attacks continues to increase. With more and more sensitive information being stored online, businesses and individuals alike are at risk of having their data compromised. Thankfully, the potential of AI in cybersecurity is immense, and it is revolutionizing the way we protect ourselves from cyber threats.

One of the key advantages of AI in cybersecurity is its ability to identify patterns. By analyzing vast amounts of data, AI algorithms can quickly identify anomalies and suspicious behavior that may indicate a cyber attack. This allows for a faster response time and more effective protection against potential threats.

Another benefit of AI in cybersecurity is its ability to learn and adapt. As cyber threats continue to evolve and become more sophisticated, traditional cybersecurity measures may not be enough to keep up. However, AI algorithms can learn from past attacks and adapt their defenses accordingly, making them more effective at protecting against future attacks.

One application of AI in cybersecurity is in threat intelligence. By analyzing data from a variety of sources, including social media, dark web forums, and hacker chats, AI algorithms can identify potential threats before they even occur. This allows for a proactive approach to cybersecurity, rather than a reactive one.

AI can also be used to automate routine cybersecurity tasks, freeing up human resources for more complex tasks. This includes tasks such as patching software vulnerabilities, managing user access privileges, and monitoring network traffic for suspicious activity. By automating these tasks, businesses can improve their cybersecurity posture without overburdening their IT staff.

However, like any technology, AI is not foolproof. Hackers are constantly finding new ways to bypass cybersecurity measures, and AI is not immune to these attacks. Additionally, there is the risk of AI algorithms being biased or making incorrect decisions based on flawed data. It is important to keep these limitations in mind when implementing AI in cybersecurity.

Overall, the potential of AI in cybersecurity is immense. By leveraging the power of AI algorithms, we can improve our ability to protect ourselves from cyber threats. However, it is important to approach the implementation of AI in cybersecurity with caution and to continuously monitor its effectiveness.

The Risks and Challenges of AI in Cybersecurity

As AI technology continues to advance, it is becoming increasingly integrated into cybersecurity systems. While there are many benefits to using AI in cybersecurity, such as improved threat detection and response times, there are also a number of risks and challenges that must be considered.

One of the biggest risks associated with AI in cybersecurity is the potential for cyber criminals to use the technology for their own advantage. For example, hackers could use AI to develop more sophisticated attacks that are better able to evade detection by traditional security measures. They could also use AI to automate attacks, allowing them to launch large-scale attacks with minimal effort.

Another challenge associated with AI in cybersecurity is the potential for false positives. While AI can be incredibly effective at detecting threats, it is also prone to making mistakes. This means that it is possible for AI systems to flag innocent behavior as malicious, leading to unnecessary alerts and wasted resources.

In addition, there is also the risk of bias in AI systems. Because AI is only as good as the data it is trained on, if that data is biased or incomplete, the resulting system will also be biased. In the case of cybersecurity, this could mean that certain types of attacks or threats are not detected as effectively as others, leaving organizations vulnerable to attack.

Finally, there is the challenge of trust. As AI becomes increasingly integrated into cybersecurity systems, there is a risk that organizations may become too reliant on the technology and fail to adequately invest in other areas of cybersecurity. This could leave them vulnerable to attacks that are not detected by AI systems, or to attacks that are able to bypass AI defenses.

In conclusion, while AI has the potential to revolutionize cybersecurity, there are also a number of risks and challenges that must be carefully considered. Organizations must be aware of these risks and invest in the necessary resources and strategies to effectively address them. By doing so, they can leverage the power of AI while also ensuring the security of their systems and data.

The Role of AI in Industries

AI in Healthcare

Artificial intelligence (AI) is revolutionizing the healthcare industry by helping clinicians and researchers to identify patterns in large data sets, diagnose diseases and predict treatment outcomes. The use of AI in healthcare has the potential to transform the field by improving patient outcomes, reducing costs and increasing efficiency.

One of the key areas where AI is making a significant impact is in medical imaging. Machine learning algorithms can analyze medical images and identify patterns that are not visible to the human eye. This technology can help radiologists to identify potential problems at an early stage, leading to earlier diagnosis and treatment. AI can also help to reduce the number of unnecessary tests and procedures, thereby reducing costs and improving patient outcomes.

AI is also being used to improve drug discovery and development. Machine learning algorithms can analyze large datasets of molecular structures and identify potential drug candidates. This technology can help researchers to identify new treatments and accelerate drug development, leading to faster approval and availability of new drugs.

Another area where AI is making an impact is in personalized medicine. By analyzing patient data, including genetic and biometric data, AI can help clinicians to develop personalized treatment plans that are tailored to the individual patient. This technology can help to improve patient outcomes and reduce the risk of adverse effects.

Cybersecurity is also an important consideration when it comes to AI in healthcare. As more patient data is stored and analyzed using AI, it is important to ensure that this information is protected from cyber threats. Strong cybersecurity measures should be put in place to protect patient data and ensure that it is not accessed by unauthorized individuals.

In conclusion, AI is rapidly transforming the healthcare industry by improving patient outcomes, reducing costs and increasing efficiency. From medical imaging to drug discovery and personalized medicine, the potential applications of AI in healthcare are vast. However, it is important to ensure that patient data is protected from cyber threats, and that strong cybersecurity measures are put in place to safeguard against potential data breaches.

AI in Finance

The integration of artificial intelligence (AI) in finance has been one of the most significant advancements in the industry. AI has the ability to process vast amounts of data at a speed and accuracy that surpasses human capabilities. This has led to the development of various applications that have significantly impacted the financial sector. In this chapter, we will explore how AI is transforming finance and its potential impact on the industry.

One of the most significant applications of AI in finance is in fraud detection and prevention. AI algorithms can identify fraudulent activities in real-time by analyzing patterns and trends in financial transactions. This has helped financial institutions save billions of dollars that would have been lost to fraudulent activities.

AI has also revolutionized investment decision-making. By analyzing vast amounts of data, AI algorithms can identify potential investment opportunities and provide insights that help investors make informed decisions. This has led to the development of robo-advisors, which are automated investment platforms that use AI algorithms to provide personalized investment advice to clients.

Another way AI is transforming finance is through the development of chatbots and virtual assistants. These tools can interact with customers and provide them with personalized financial advice. This has led to the development of digital banks that offer 24/7 customer service and personalized financial advice.

While AI has numerous benefits in finance, there are also concerns about its potential impact. One of the major concerns is the potential loss of jobs due to automation. However, experts believe that the integration of AI will create new job opportunities that require specialized skills in data analysis and machine learning.

Another concern is cybersecurity. Financial institutions hold vast amounts of sensitive data, and the integration of AI could increase the risk of cyber-attacks. However, experts are working to develop cybersecurity solutions that use AI to detect and prevent cyber-attacks.

In conclusion, AI has the potential to revolutionize finance by improving fraud detection and prevention, investment decision-making, and customer service. While there are concerns about its potential impact, experts believe that the benefits of AI in finance far outweigh the risks. As such, financial institutions must embrace AI to remain competitive in an increasingly digital world.

AI in Education

AI in Education

Artificial intelligence (AI) is transforming education in ways that were previously unimaginable. AI technology is being used to personalize learning experiences, improve retention rates, and enhance student engagement. AI-powered tools are helping educators create more effective lesson plans, identify areas where students need more support, and provide real-time feedback to students.

One of the most significant benefits of AI in education is personalization. Using algorithms and machine learning, AI technology can analyze student data to create personalized learning experiences that meet the unique needs of each student. This technology can take into account a student's learning style, preferences, and strengths and weaknesses to create a customized curriculum.

AI can also help educators identify areas where students need more support. For example, AI-powered tools can analyze student performance data to identify patterns and trends that may indicate a need for additional instruction or support. This information can be used to create targeted interventions that help students overcome academic challenges.

Another benefit of AI in education is improved retention rates. AI-powered tools can help students stay engaged and motivated by providing real-time feedback and support. This can help prevent students from falling behind or dropping out of school.

However, as with any technology, there are also concerns about cybersecurity when it comes to AI in education. Personalized learning experiences require a significant amount of student data to be collected and analyzed. This data must be protected to ensure that student privacy is maintained.

In conclusion, AI technology is transforming education in exciting ways. From personalized learning experiences to improved retention rates, AI-powered tools are helping educators create more effective lesson plans and support student success. However, it is important to ensure that student privacy is protected and cybersecurity measures are in place to safeguard student data. As AI technology continues to evolve, its potential in education will only continue to grow.

AI in Retail

AI in Retail

In recent years, the retail industry has undergone a massive transformation, thanks to the rise of artificial intelligence technologies. AI has enabled retailers to better understand their customers, improve their operations, and increase their sales. In this subchapter, we will explore how AI is revolutionizing the retail industry and what this means for the future of retail.

One of the most significant benefits of AI in retail is the ability to provide personalized shopping experiences for customers. With AI, retailers can collect and analyze vast amounts of data from various sources, including social media, online browsing behavior, and transaction history. This data can then be used to create personalized recommendations, offers, and promotions that are tailored to each customer's preferences and needs.

AI is also transforming the supply chain and logistics aspects of retail. By using predictive analytics, retailers can optimize their inventory management, reducing the risk of overstocking or underselling. AI-powered robots and drones are also being used for order fulfillment and delivery, reducing the need for human labor and improving efficiency.

However, the adoption of AI in retail also poses significant challenges, particularly in the area of cybersecurity. Retailers must ensure that the data they collect and store is secure and protected from cyber threats. This means investing in robust cybersecurity measures, including encryption, multi-factor authentication, and intrusion detection systems.

Another concern is the potential impact of AI on employment in the retail industry. While AI-powered systems can improve efficiency and reduce costs, they also have the potential to displace human workers. Retailers must balance the benefits of AI with the need to maintain a skilled workforce and ensure that workers are trained and equipped with the skills required to work alongside AI-powered systems.

In conclusion, the rise of AI in retail is transforming the industry, and its impact will only continue to grow in the coming years. While there are challenges and concerns associated with the adoption of AI in retail, the benefits are undeniable. Retailers that embrace AI and use it to enhance customer experiences, optimize operations, and increase sales will be well-positioned for success in the future.

AI in Transportation

AI in Transportation

The transportation industry is one of the largest and most critical sectors of the global economy. It comprises various modes of transportation such as aviation, maritime, rail, road, and public transportation, which are responsible for moving goods and people from one place to another. With the advent of artificial intelligence (AI), the transportation industry is set to experience a significant transformation. AI technology promises to revolutionize the way we travel, commute, and transport goods by making transportation safer, faster, and more efficient.

One of the most significant impacts of AI on transportation is the development of self-driving vehicles. Autonomous vehicles (AVs) are equipped with advanced sensors and machine learning algorithms that enable them to navigate roads, avoid obstacles, and make decisions without human intervention. AVs have the potential to reduce accidents, traffic congestion, and carbon emissions, making transportation more eco-friendly and sustainable.

Another application of AI in transportation is predictive maintenance. AI algorithms can analyze data from sensors installed in vehicles and predict when a vehicle component is likely to fail. This can help transportation companies schedule maintenance proactively, reducing downtime and improving vehicle reliability. Predictive maintenance can also save costs by avoiding unscheduled maintenance and reducing the need for spare parts.

AI can also improve the efficiency of transportation logistics. AI algorithms can optimize route planning, load balancing, and delivery scheduling, reducing transit times and improving delivery accuracy. This can help logistics companies save costs and improve customer satisfaction.

However, with the increased use of AI in transportation, there are also concerns about cybersecurity. As AI systems become more integrated into transportation systems, they become vulnerable to cyber-attacks. Hackers can exploit vulnerabilities in AI algorithms to gain access to critical transportation systems, causing accidents and disruptions. Therefore, it is crucial to ensure that AI systems used in transportation are secure and resilient to cyber threats.

In conclusion, AI technology has the potential to transform the transportation industry by making transportation safer, faster, and more efficient. However, to realize the full potential of AI in transportation, it is essential to address cybersecurity concerns and ensure that AI systems are secure and resilient. The future of transportation is exciting, and AI is set to play a significant role in shaping it.

AI in Manufacturing

AI in Manufacturing

The manufacturing industry has always been at the forefront of technological advancements. From steam engines to assembly lines, manufacturers have always looked for ways to automate and streamline their operations. In the past few years, AI has emerged as a game changer in the manufacturing industry. The ability of AI systems to process large amounts of data and make predictions based on that data has made them invaluable in optimizing manufacturing processes.

One of the most significant benefits of AI in manufacturing is its ability to improve efficiency. AI systems can analyze data from sensors, machines, and other sources to identify patterns and anomalies. This information can then be used to optimize production processes, reduce downtime, and improve quality. For example, an AI system can analyze data from sensors on a production line to identify which machines are likely to fail. This information can then be used to schedule maintenance before a breakdown occurs, reducing downtime and increasing efficiency.

Another area where AI can benefit the manufacturing industry is in quality control. AI systems can analyze images of products to identify defects and anomalies. This information can then be used to improve the manufacturing process and reduce the number of defective products. For example, an AI system can analyze images of electronic components to identify defects that are too small to be seen by the human eye. This information can then be used to improve the manufacturing process and reduce the number of defective components.

However, as with any technology, there are also risks associated with AI in manufacturing. Cybersecurity is a major concern, as AI systems can be vulnerable to cyber attacks. For example, an attacker could manipulate data fed into an AI system, causing it to make incorrect predictions. This could lead to defective products or even safety hazards. Therefore, it is essential that manufacturers implement robust cybersecurity measures to protect their AI systems.

In conclusion, AI has the potential to revolutionize the manufacturing industry. Its ability to analyze large amounts of data and make predictions based on that data can help manufacturers optimize their processes, improve quality, and reduce downtime. However, it is also important to be aware of the risks associated with AI and to implement robust cybersecurity measures to protect against cyber attacks. As the manufacturing industry continues to evolve, it is clear that AI will play an increasingly important role in shaping its future.

Implementing AI in Business

Steps to Implementing AI in Business

The implementation of artificial intelligence (AI) in business has become a hot topic in recent years. With the potential to streamline processes, increase efficiency, and drive profitability, it's no wonder that businesses are keen to adopt AI technology. However, implementing AI in business is not as simple as flipping a switch. It requires careful planning, consideration, and execution. In this subchapter, we will discuss the steps to implementing AI in business.

Step 1: Define the Problem

The first step in implementing AI in business is to define the problem you want to solve. AI can be applied to a broad range of business problems, from automating processes to improving customer experience. Once you have identified the problem, you can begin to determine what type of AI technology will be most effective.

Step 2: Gather Data

AI requires vast amounts of data to function effectively. Therefore, the second step in implementing AI in business is to gather data. This includes both structured and unstructured data from various sources, such as customer data, sales data, and social media data.

Step 3: Choose the Right AI Technology

There are many different types of AI technology, such as machine learning and natural language processing. Choosing the right technology for your business problem is critical to achieving success. It's important to consider factors such as the complexity of the problem, the type of data you have, and the level of expertise required to implement and maintain the technology.

Step 4: Develop and Train the AI Model

Once you have chosen the right AI technology, the next step is to develop and train the AI model. This involves selecting the algorithms and frameworks to use, building the model, and training it using the data you have gathered.

Step 5: Implement and Monitor the AI Model
The final step in implementing AI in business is to implement and monitor the AI model. This involves integrating the model into your business processes, monitoring its performance, and making adjustments as needed.

In conclusion, implementing AI in business requires careful planning, consideration, and execution. By following the steps outlined in this subchapter, businesses can successfully implement AI technology to streamline processes, increase efficiency, and drive profitability. However, it's important to remember that implementing AI is an ongoing process that requires continuous monitoring and adjustments to ensure success.

Overcoming Challenges in Implementing AI

As businesses continue to embrace the power of Artificial Intelligence (AI), they face challenges in implementing it effectively. Despite the potential benefits of AI, there are significant obstacles that need to be overcome to ensure successful implementation. Here are some of the challenges businesses face and how to overcome them.

1. Data quality and availability

AI systems rely on high-quality data to make accurate predictions and decisions. However, many businesses struggle to maintain the quality of their data, which can lead to inaccurate results. Additionally, some businesses may not have access to the necessary data, making it difficult to implement AI effectively.

To overcome this challenge, businesses need to invest in data management and quality control processes. This includes ensuring that data is accurate, complete, and up-to-date. Additionally, businesses should consider partnering with data providers to gain access to the necessary data to drive AI initiatives.

2. Cybersecurity risks

AI systems can be vulnerable to cyber threats, such as hacking and data breaches. These risks can lead to significant financial and reputational damage, making cybersecurity a critical consideration in AI implementation.

To mitigate these risks, businesses should implement robust cybersecurity measures, including encryption, access controls, and monitoring. Additionally, businesses should regularly test their AI systems for vulnerabilities and ensure that all stakeholders are aware of cybersecurity risks and best practices.

3. Bias and ethical considerations

AI systems can be biased if they are trained on biased data or developed by biased individuals. This can result in unfair outcomes, such as discrimination, and damage a company's reputation.

To address this challenge, businesses should ensure that their AI systems are developed and trained using diverse data sets and by a diverse team of experts. Additionally, businesses should consider the ethical implications of their AI initiatives and ensure that they align with their values and mission.

In conclusion, while implementing AI can be challenging, businesses can overcome these obstacles by investing in data quality and management, robust cybersecurity measures, and ethical considerations. By doing so, businesses can unlock the full potential of AI and drive innovation and growth in the future.

The Future of AI Implementation in Business

As we move further into the 21st century, it is evident that artificial intelligence (AI) is set to revolutionize the business landscape. Companies across various industries are already harnessing the power of AI to improve their operations, enhance customer experiences and boost their bottom lines. With the rapid advancements in AI technology, it is clear that the future of AI implementation in business is bright.

One of the most significant benefits of AI in business is increased efficiency. AI-powered systems can automate repetitive tasks, freeing up employees to focus on more complex and creative work. This, in turn, leads to more productivity and better use of resources. For instance, in the healthcare sector, AI-powered systems can analyze vast amounts of data to assist physicians in making more accurate diagnoses and creating personalized treatment plans. This could lead to better outcomes for patients while reducing the workload on healthcare professionals.

Another area where AI is set to make significant strides is in cybersecurity. Cybersecurity threats are becoming more complex and sophisticated, and traditional security measures may no longer be enough. AI can be used to identify potential attacks before they happen and respond to them in real-time. AI can also be used to analyze vast amounts of data to identify patterns and detect anomalies that may indicate a security breach. This could help businesses stay ahead of potential cybersecurity threats and protect their sensitive data.

In the coming years, AI is also expected to transform the way businesses interact with their customers. AI-powered chatbots, for instance, can provide personalized and timely responses to customer queries, improving customer satisfaction. AI can also be used to analyze customer data to provide more personalized recommendations and offers, leading to more sales and revenue.

However, as with any technological advancement, there are also concerns around the future of AI implementation in business. One of the biggest concerns is the potential impact on jobs. While AI can automate repetitive tasks, it could also lead to job losses in certain sectors. It is crucial for businesses to consider the ethical implications of AI implementation and ensure that they are using the technology responsibly.

In conclusion, the future of AI implementation in business is exciting, and companies that embrace this technology are likely to reap significant benefits. However, it is crucial for businesses to approach AI implementation with caution and ensure that they are using the technology in an ethical and responsible manner. As AI continues to evolve, it is clear that it will play an increasingly important role in shaping the future of businesses worldwide.

Conclusion

Recap of Key Points

Recap of Key Points

Throughout this book, we have explored some of the most critical aspects of the future of AI and how it will change business forever. We have seen how machine learning is already transforming every aspect of the industry, from customer service to manufacturing and logistics. In this final section, we will recap some of the key points we have discussed throughout the book.

Firstly, we have seen that AI technology is rapidly advancing and becoming more accessible to businesses of all sizes. It is no longer just the domain of large corporations and tech giants. Small and medium-sized businesses can now use AI to gain a competitive edge and streamline their operations.

Secondly, we have discussed how AI technology is transforming customer service. Chatbots are becoming increasingly sophisticated and can now handle complex queries and provide personalized recommendations to customers. This has the potential to significantly improve customer satisfaction and reduce costs for businesses.

Thirdly, we have looked at how AI is changing the way we manufacture and distribute goods. With the use of machine learning algorithms, manufacturers can optimize their production processes for increased efficiency and accuracy. This leads to cost savings and faster delivery times.

Fourthly, we have discussed how AI is being used to improve cybersecurity. With the increasing threat of cyber-attacks, AI technology is becoming a critical tool in detecting and preventing cyber threats. Machine learning algorithms can analyze vast amounts of data and identify patterns that indicate a potential breach.

In conclusion, the future of AI is exciting, and it is clear that it will continue to revolutionize the way we do business. However, it is essential to recognize that AI technology also poses significant challenges, particularly around data privacy and job displacement. As AI continues to evolve, we must ensure that we are using it in an ethical and responsible way that benefits society as a whole.

Final Thoughts on the Future of AI and Machine Learning in Business

Final Thoughts on the Future of AI and

Machine Learning in Business

As we have explored in this book, AI and machine learning are already transforming the business landscape in remarkable ways. From automating routine tasks to enabling advanced analytics and predictive modeling, these technologies are helping companies to work faster, smarter, and more efficiently. However, this is just the beginning of what is possible.

Looking ahead, we can expect to see AI and machine learning continue to evolve and improve, becoming even more sophisticated and capable of handling increasingly complex tasks. This will open up new opportunities for businesses to innovate and grow, but it will also create new challenges and risks that need to be addressed.

One of the most significant challenges that businesses will face is the need to keep up with the rapid pace of technological change. As AI and machine learning continue to advance, companies must be prepared to adapt and evolve their strategies and operations to stay competitive. This will require ongoing investment in research, development, and training, as well as a willingness to embrace new technologies and ways of working.

Another challenge for businesses will be ensuring the security and privacy of their data and systems. As AI and machine learning become more widespread, they will become increasingly attractive targets for cyber criminals and hackers. Companies must therefore invest in robust cybersecurity measures and develop strategies for managing and mitigating the risks associated with these technologies.

Despite these challenges, however, the future of AI and machine learning in business is bright. By leveraging these technologies effectively, companies can gain a competitive edge, improve efficiency, and drive innovation. As we move forward, it is important for businesses to stay informed and engaged with the latest developments in AI and machine learning, and to be proactive in exploring their potential applications and benefits.

Ultimately, the future of AI and machine learning in business will be shaped by the collective efforts of companies, researchers, policymakers, and other stakeholders. By working together, we can ensure that these technologies are used in ways that are responsible, ethical, and beneficial for all.

Call to Action for Businesses to Embrace AI.

The future of business lies in the integration of Artificial Intelligence (AI) technology. The use of AI in business is no longer a matter of if, but when. It is imperative that businesses embrace AI technology to remain competitive in the market and keep up with the changing times.

The benefits of AI technology in business are numerous. Businesses can use AI to analyze consumer behavior, predict market trends, and optimize supply chains. AI can also be used to automate mundane tasks, freeing up human resources to focus on more creative and strategic tasks.

One of the primary reasons businesses have been slow to adopt AI technology is the fear of job loss. However, studies have shown that the integration of AI technology will actually create new job opportunities, while also improving the efficiency and productivity of existing jobs.

Another concern is the potential security risks associated with AI technology. However, this can be mitigated through the implementation of proper cybersecurity protocols and the use of ethical AI practices.

It is crucial for businesses to embrace AI technology to remain competitive and relevant in today's market. Companies that fail to do so risk falling behind their competitors and losing market share. The call to action for businesses is clear: embrace AI technology or risk being left behind.

In conclusion, AI technology is the future of business. It has the potential to revolutionize the way we do business and provide numerous benefits to companies of all sizes. The time to embrace AI technology is now, and businesses must take action to remain competitive and relevant in the ever-changing business landscape.